DEPT. OF HOME ECONOMICS
AND
SOCIAL WORK STUDIES

Hair-Styles and Head-Dresses

Renée Huggett

Batsford Academic and Educational Ltd London

Typeset by Tek-Art, London SE20
and printed in Great Britain by
R.J. Acford
Chichester, Sussex
for the publishers
Batsford Academic and Educational Ltd,
an imprint of B T Batsford Ltd,
4 Fitzhardinge Street
London W1H 0AH

ISBN 0 7134 4067 8

ACKNOWLEDGMENT

The Author and Publishers would like to thank the following for their kind permission to reproduce copyright illustrations: Ashmolean Museum, Oxford, fig 26; Blandford Press, fig 43 (from *Costume and Fashion 1760-1920* by Jack Cassin-Scott, 1971); Bodleian Library, Oxford, fig 13, The British Library, figs 11, 12, 16, 28, 29, 31, 36, 45, 47, 48, 50, 52, 55, 56, 57, 58; *The Connoisseur*, figs 32, 33; Dover Publications, figs 1, 5, 9, 19, 39; *Hairdressers Journal International*, figs 62, 63, 64, 65, 66; Pat Hodgson Picture Library, figs 7, 8, 10, 14, 15, 30, 34, 38, 42; Mansell Collection, figs 2, 3, 4, 17, 20, 21, 24, 25, 35, 37, 40, 41; William Morris Gallery, Walthamstow, fig 49; National Portrait Gallery, London, figs 23, 61; Royal Academy of Arts, fig 18; Tate Gallery, London, fig 44; John Topham Picture Library, fig 60; Victoria and Albert Museum, figs 22, 46. Figs 53, 54 and 59 were specially drawn by P.B. Raymond, Raymond Art de Coiffure Ltd.

Contents

The
Illustrations

Introduction

Mankind seems always to have been aware of the importance of a beautiful head of hair and the dressing of the hair goes back to earliest recorded history.

Cavemen and neanderthal man and even stone age men may have worn their hair long and unadorned for warmth, but as soon as human beings began to live in permanent groups the head seems to have been recognized as the most important part of the individual in his contact with the outside world. Long before men knew that the head was the repository of the brain, primitive man painted his face or created masks representing the animals or devils he feared, either to ward off danger or to emulate their powers.

To a certain extent, even the simplest head-dress relies upon the use of tools and the simplest hair-style requires cutting or some kind of equipment to keep it in place.

But, in spite of this, all ancient civilizations went to great lengths to have elaborate hair-styles and head-dresses -- even greater than with fashions in clothes.

Neither the hair-style nor the head-dress worn was the result of an individual decision. It did not depend upon personal caprice or preference.

The emergence of leaders and therefore of decision-makers seems to be a part of the development of the human race. No group can be equal. In early times, the leader of a group was probably the one who was the strongest, the fastest or the best at warding off evil spirits. The witch doctor and magic man must have been the first leaders of mankind. By the time the earliest civilizations emerged in the Middle and Far East, those natural leaders had also become the wealth holders. Added to their decision-making role,

1   Although men and women already wore jewellery in the Bronze Age, they had not started to style their hair, which was usually worn long and straight.

this created a pattern of power which has not changed in any civilization since. The leadership role depends upon a variety of attributes from superior intelligence, strength or imagination to less desirable qualities such as violence or greed, but it always carries with it the ability to lead, dominate and influence one's fellow human beings. Having these qualities, the leaders naturally accumulate to themselves the wealth of their particular society, whether it be in money, land, cattle or objects of art. In all societies, the leaders not only attracted wealth to themselves. Their resulting power gave them the opportunity also to govern. They made the laws, and in every civilization we shall find that those in power have either created fashions or controlled them.

This power, of many different kinds, has been held by different groups in different eras and civilizations, from the priests of ancient Egypt to the European courts of the eighteenth century and the film stars of the 1930s. They were all people with the wealth and power to influence others.

We shall see, therefore, that hair-styles have always been a reflection of the society in which they were created. Even today, evidence of our belief in the freedom of the individual is shown in the variety and the extremes of hair-styles worn. But the actual styles are still created by the "trend-setters" who are pop-singers, society people, or famous fashion designers, because one aspect of twentieth-century power lies in the ability and the opportunity to influence the media.

1
Hair in Ancient Times

In modern times, hair has always been a girl's — and now a boy's — crowning glory, but in ancient civilizations, head-dresses were of much greater importance than the hair itself.

Ancient Egypt

More than three thousand years before the birth of Christ, the ancient Egyptians were wearing elaborate head-dresses representing the sacred animals which they both feared and worshipped.

Religion has often had a great influence upon the kinds of head-dresses that people wear, and also on hair-styles. This influence was very strong in ancient Egypt, where the priests and the Pharaohs exercised dominant power for many thousands of years.

In Egypt an elaborate system of worship developed which is illustrated in the many paintings in their tombs and temples. The Egyptians worshipped about two thousand gods and deities, most of them representing animals, birds and even trees. Head-dresses, in the shape of jackals, rams, lions and many other animals, were one of the most important features of their religious rites. They were made of many materials, such as linen or stiffened leather, painted in gold with jewelled decorations and all of them had symbolic and magical meanings. The Pharaohs

2   The plaited wigs worn by the Egyptians can be seen, surmounted by emblems of vultures, which were made of gold.

wore a magnificent head-dress depicting Osiris, the god of the dead. It consisted of a curled or plaited wig, surmounted by a gold emblem of a vulture and cobra.

7

3   Fashionable girls in ancient Egypt wore cones of fat on the top of their heads so that, as the fat melted, it kept the hair-style in place. The servant girl is helping them to dress.

Many head-dresses were so heavy and cumbersome that it was necessary to shave the head to keep them on. Even women cut their hair very short or shaved it off altogether so that they could wear the elaborate head-dresses on religious and ceremonial occasions. At other times, they felt rather naked with their shaven heads and so they took to wearing wigs indoors and outdoors. These were also intended to protect them against the fierce rays of the sun, but it must have been very hot to wear them, despite their shaven heads.

The wigs were set in a rigid style. There was no parting and they were closely curled, often with long ringlets. Sometimes they were coiled and plaited and spiked with embossed gold. The long hair which is depicted in tomb paintings is always a wig, often with braids falling to the breasts. Sometimes the wig was cut short and square and this style was worn by both men and women. As time passed, it became fashionable to have long hair at the back, some of it falling over the shoulders in the front.

To keep the hair-style — or wig-style — in place, a cone of perfumed fat was stuck on top of the wig. This melted in the heat of the sun and ran down over the wig like candle wax. It not only kept the hair of the wig in place but had the added attraction of making it shine.

For probably two thousand years — longer than our own Christian civilization — Egyptian hair-styles did not change very much. In about 1500 BC fringes became popular but these were still usually part of the wig. Men had a bob and fringe and women had long hair at the back. As time passed, it became more customary to let your own hair grow, but the fringe still persisted and the real hair was often interwoven with the wig.

The head-dress was worn on top of the wig and in the Egyptian climate this must have made the wigs feel even more hot and uncomfortable.

The fashion for head-dresses was not confined to Egypt. In Babylon four thousand years ago, men also wore head-dresses and they were the first people to wear helmets.

Many other ancient civilizations adopted the wig. The Chaldean men wore wigs, but the women wore hoods which gradually developed into more elaborate head-dresses, consisting of gold wire with beads and flowers and precious stones interwoven with little animals in gold.

Ancient Greece

The dressing and styling of a person's own hair started much later — in ancient Athens. The Greeks and Romans had very different conventions from the earlier civilizations of the Middle East. The power did not rest absolutely with the priesthood, but with wealthy citizens. While the gods dominated their imagination, their daily lives were based upon a humanistic art and culture, even if it was only for a minority of freemen and not for the benefit of the thousands of slaves.

Their gods were supermen and heroes, idealized versions of the human form. As a result, they wore neither head-dress nor wigs. With the Egyptians, the head-dress was not meant to enhance the individual's appearance but to placate the gods. The ancient Greeks were immensely interested, on the other hand, in personal and particularly masculine beauty.

Men wore their hair short but it gradually became fashionable to wear it waist-length. There was also a fashion for dividing each lock of hair into curls and ringlets.

Women wore their hair in an informal style which has been popular in practically all eras ever since. The hair was worn long and loose, either not curled or only lightly waved, sometimes with part of the hair drawn back into a chignon, the rest falling over the back and shoulders. It is probably the style most admired by romantic writers and artists and is still as popular today.

4   A King of Assyria. Elaborately curled wigs and beards were worn by rulers in many ancient civilizations, as a sign of their status.

9

Later, Greek men wore caps or wound their long hair round their heads. They also began to experiment with different styles. They cut their hair in a fringe with a twist of hair at the back turned upwards, with curls hanging loosely over their shoulders, or they had a curled fringe with a pony tail. They combed their hair forward in a fringe, plaited it at the back, wore ringlets at each side of their ears and curled their beards. Later, they wore their hair hanging down the back and tied with a ribbon, with ringlets on either side of the head.

Women also experimented with their own hair instead of covering it with a wig. Curls over the forehead were very popular. They also gathered their hair into a knot on top of the head.

Ancient Rome

The ancient Romans were even more fashion-conscious about their hair. The fashion leaders were the wealthy emperors, their families and friends. There was also a large number of wealthy citizens who, particularly in the later years of the empire, devoted their lives to pleasure.

One of the most distinctive hair-styles of Roman men was a style which lasted for about six hundred years. This was a method of cutting the hair in a circle and turning it inwards all round the head. This style was copied by the Britons during the Roman occupation of this country.

For Roman women, attending to their hair was one of their main activities and slaves were specially trained to do the hair-dressing.

Hairdressing gradually became a greatly admired profession and in the later years of the Roman empire, wigs were re-introduced, which gave further scope for fashion and invention.

Some Romans were so keen to have everything in their homes in the latest fashion that one wealthy citizen had a statue made with interchangeable wigs, made of stone, so that the individual would never be out of fashion. It can still be seen in the Louvre Museum in Paris.

Octavia, the daughter of Claudius and the wife of the famous Emperor Nero, introduced a fashion for a centre parting and a chignon.

Messalina, who married Claudius when she was fifteen, preferred curls and waves and there was also a fashion for tying the hair in a red or purple band.

Hadrian started a fashion for men by crimping his hair in tight waves, and beards also re-appeared in his reign.

5   Roman women liked to style their own hair instead of covering it with a wig. Curls and chignons at the back were popular. The slave girl's hair (right) is hidden. She would not have been allowed to copy the hair-styles of the higher ranks in society.

Hairdressing Equipment

In Egypt, Greece and Rome, primitive curling tongs were used, and colouring the hair is also as old as civilization.

The Greeks dyed their hair blonde and powdered it with gold dust. The Romans used a liquid dye, prepared from leaches. It was left for sixty days to purify and was then plastered on the hair.

Golden hair was also fashionable among Roman women and saffron was used to make it yellow. They also believed that standing bareheaded in the sun would bleach their hair and they spent many hours in the heat, although this must have been a slow process. Many women simply cut off their dark hair and wore a blonde wig.

Long and Short Hair

It is interesting to note that in early times, the way in which the hair was dressed and cut had different meanings for different races. It was not styled merely for beauty; it also had symbolic meanings, and certain hair-styles were reserved for different groups in society.

The length of the hair seems always to have had the most significance. Caesar is said to have made the Gauls cut off their hair when he conquered France, as a sign of submission. It has always been customary for monks to cut their hair short or to shave their heads because long hair was also associated with vanity. In all Greek civilizations it was essential to have really short hair as a sign of mourning for a dead relative, and the long hair of Greek children was cut off in adolescence to indicate the approach of adulthood.

Long hair, on the other hand, was associated with strength. In the Bible story of Samson and Delilah, Delilah cuts off Samson's hair while he is sleeping and, as a result, he loses all his strength. There has also been a tendency for long hair for women to be associated with innocence and purity. In some civilizations, such as the Greeks in the centuries before Christ, long hair for a man indicated that he was a peasant. Those higher up on the social scale wore their hair short and combed down. In fact, slaves were never allowed to wear the same hair-style as their masters, whatever might be the current fashion.

It was to be many centuries before people could wear their hair as they pleased.

11

2
Early British Hair-Styles

The ancient Greeks and the Romans had had the wealth and time to lavish attention on their hair. But with the invasions of the Teutonic tribes and the ultimate collapse of the Roman empire, western Europe declined into anarchy.

When we turn to Europe in the early centuries after Christ, we find that the backwardness in their civilization is reflected also in their hair and dress.

Power now lay not with the leaders of a settled community but with the invaders and marauders, intent on plunder or on building up an empire. These people were more concerned with survival and exploitation and had little time for fashion or luxury. In Britain, both men and women wore their hair long and loose and this style continued almost until the Norman Conquest.

There were no wigs and no kind of headdress. King Canute (995-1035), who is reputed to have tried to stop the sea coming in, is always depicted with hair falling over his shoulders in great profusion.

The Anglo-Saxons were very proud of their long hair, however, particularly if it was fair or yellow, which distinguished them from the dark-haired Mediterranean people whom they had defeated in war. To enhance the natural fashionable colour, they dyed their hair with tallow, mixed with ashes of vegetables. They also coloured the curls on their forehead sky-blue or some-times green. Beards were often coloured blue as well. In some Anglo-Saxon manuscripts, the hair is shown as bright red and sometimes green or orange. It is not known whether this was done with a dye or a powder.

Although the Anglo-Saxons had long hair, it had to be cut off when they married. Presumably, it was allowed to grow long again afterwards. No Saxon woman had her hair showing. Her head and neck were covered with a hood or veil and even in the house the veil was still worn.

After the Norman Conquest, a new power began to develop and the representatives of the Christian Church had an increasing influence on people's lives. The early Christian Church was very different from the earlier religions. The leaders did not believe in adorning themselves for the glory of their gods, or to gain their protection, as the Egyptians had. The Christian god was interpreted by the clergy as being severe and righteous, opposed to any form of vanity or pleasure. Wealth might be expended on magnificent churches and monasteries, but human adornment was sinful. Throughout most of its history, the Christian Church seems always to have associated long hair with sin and vice.

In 1096 the leaders of the Church, which was then, of course, the Church of Rome, banned long hair for all members of the

6   After the Norman Conquest, English women wore more formal head-dress. This lady is wearing a barbette, even while milking the cows. It was a style which continued to be worn for about two hundred years.

congregation. The clergy themselves shaved the crowns of their heads and had a circular tonsure, which was deemed to be morally preferable to growing their own hair.

Earlier, St Wulstan, who lived in the reign of Edward the Confessor (c. 1002-1066), had been even more positive in his approach. He condemned the wicked "of all ranks" who were proud of their long hair. When they bowed to receive his blessing he would cut off a lock of their hair with a sharp little knife which he carried around for that purpose. They were then told to go home and cut off the rest.

In fact, long hair became an obsession with the clergy. Anselm, Archbishop of Canterbury from 1093 to 1109, pronounced sentence of excommunication against all those with long hair.

A Norman bishop preached a sermon against long hair for men to Henry I, who reigned from 1100 to 1135. He also included

7   Queen Matilda, wife of Henry I, helped to make long plaits more fashionable from the beginning of the twelfth century.

13

in his condemnation the curling of hair. The Church was so powerful in those days, even in relation to kings, that Henry did as he was told and had his hair cut off. He then issued an edict banning the wearing of long hair for all men.

In 1129 a knight is said to have dreamed that he was suffocated by his own long curls. The nightmare was so vivid that afterwards he had his hair cut off. This started a fashion among the knights, who all followed suit.

Stephen, who reigned after Henry I, also had his hair cut short. But in spite of the endless criticism and censure of the clergy, many people still wanted to grow their hair long. From about 1135 wigs began to be worn, but the clergy turned out to be as opposed to wigs as they were to long hair.

8   The influence of the Church in the Norman period forced men to wear their hair short and women to cover their heads.

14

3
The Mediaeval Period

The Middle Ages saw the gradual development of Europe and, with the increase in wealth and a leisured class, we have the beginnings of hair-styles and head-dresses in the west.

There was, however, a significant difference. Fashion in Egyptian times was not connected with individual beauty or vanity. The head-dress was rather like a uniform worn in the service of the gods. Mediaeval fashions, on the other hand, were meant to make you look beautiful. The ideal of feminine beauty began at this time. The Church continued to criticize and condemn vanity, but with notable lack of success.

The fashions were very similar in all countries, passing from one royal head to another, to be imitated by the court and those with sufficient time and money.

Hair-styles began very simply in the twelfth century. For about three centuries, women of royal birth and unmarried girls tended to wear their hair long and loose. Sometimes it was very long, reaching down to the waist. Ordinary men continued to wear their hair combed downwards around the head, as they had done in Roman times.

Until the thirteenth century, the only head-dress worn by men was a round band.

But from the beginning of the twelfth century, women began to change their attitude towards their hair and it was they who first rebelled against the kill-joy dictates

9   Elaborate head-dresses began to be worn for the first time in England in the fifteenth century. The hair was often plaited and coiled round the head.

of the male clergy. For centuries, women had had their heads covered, swathed in a hood or veil, with material draped round their necks. Then plaits began to be worn and as these grew longer, women started for the first time to leave their heads uncovered.

Long plaits became so popular that they sometimes reached to the ground and women who were unable to achieve this length attached metal rolls to the end of the plaits to make them look longer. They also began to use false hair, both human and animal, to plait with their own hair to make it look thicker.

This long-hair fashion lasted for only about twenty years, probably because of the difficulty of growing hair so long, and by the middle of the twelfth century hair was partly hidden once again beneath a veil, although young girls continued to wear their hair long and loose and uncovered.

But women's desire for adornment was so great that they started wearing head-dresses, which needed hair to support them.

The barbette was a band of material which was tied around the face and under the chin like a bandage and only a small amount of hair would have been showing on the crown.

But the wimple, which appeared at the

10   The wimple was worn by all classes of society, even nuns, in the fifteenth century.

end of the twelfth century, was a strip of silk draped around the throat and attached to the hair on top of the head. At first, the hair was completely concealed, because a veil was put on top of the wimple. But as the years passed, short plaits became popular and the wimple was attached to the plaits on each side of the face. The plaits were worn at various angles around the face supported by wires. A net was put over the plaits, reminiscent of Egyptian hair-styles, with its gold thread and jewels, the mixture of real and false hair and its rather severe lines.

Plaits were also coiled over the ears and fixed vertically on each side of the face. The jewelled nets covering the plaits and holding them in place were sometimes replaced by material.

A silk bag, embroidered with gold and jewels was made to fit over the plaits. Nets and veils such as had been used in ancient Egypt now re-appeared in the Middle Ages.

The wimple was very popular because it made almost any hair-style look attractive and it continued to be worn for about two hundred years. The fillet, which had been worn by women in ancient Greece, also re-appeared. This band of linen or silk, worn round the crown of the head and over the forehead, can still be seen in many parts of the world today, particularly in America and Southern Europe.

Influenced perhaps by women's rebellion, men in the thirteenth century also began to spend more time on their hair. They wore it very thick and bushy and then began to curl it. The curls gradually became larger and were pressed tightly on each side of the face. In the Prologue to the *Canterbury Tales*, the fourteenth-century poet, Chaucer, mentions that the hair of the Young Squire was curled as if it had been laid in a press.

Fringes also became popular and some men wore the front hair in a roll. Sometimes men wore a skull cap and at night a velvet band round their heads. This was probably as much for warmth as for decoration in the unheated bedrooms of those days.

hair was really an encumbrance and was probably cut as short as possible.

The elaborate head-dress began early in the fifteenth century when a roll of hair was pinned to the crown of the head. This roll gradually became larger and larger and the head-dress became taller and taller. Some of the head-dresses were made of metal of various shapes and sizes and must have been very unpleasant to wear. Added to this were rolls of velvet, embroidered with jewels, veils and nets.

The most popular were the horned head-dress, the butterfly, the hennin and the heart-shaped. Although today they look like something you might wear to a fancy-dress ball, they are evidence that in the fifteenth century western Europe was developing into a more sophisticated society. To the people then, the head-dresses were a sign of elegance, wealth and culture.

11 In another fifteenth-century style, the hair was worn loose at the back and the rest was plaited, but concealed beneath jewelled or embroidered ear-covers.

12 Horned head-dresses, worn by the lady in front of the fire, started to be replaced by the sugar loaf in the fifteenth century.

The fourteenth century still favoured plaits for women, with hair parted in the middle and the plaits bound round with silk braids. Sometimes a wig was used, in which the hair was plaited and decorated, and simply placed over the wearer's own hair.

Until the end of the century, nets and silks continued to be used to conceal or adorn the hair, sometimes covered with a linen veil. The nets were made of gold or silver cloth and covered with jewels.

But, at the same time, the fashion for veils meant that many women covered their heads completely, and by the fifteenth century the hair was once more completely hidden and women concentrated on head-dresses again.

As a result, the head-dress became more and more elaborate and a large part of a woman's day must have been devoted to getting it fitted on her head. For many years, the head-dress took the place of hair; the

13 Examples of the various head-dresses popular in the fifteenth century.

The horned head-dress which appeared in about 1420 was shaped, as its name implies, like the horns of a cow, but there all similarity ends, because the horns were padded and from the wires which supported them hung a veil. A metal frame on either side of the face was decorated with jewels and embroidery. The hair was pushed into a net cap which was also ornamented, so that the hair was not visible at all. In order to ensure this, women shaved their front hair above the forehead, which was supposed to give them added beauty. They also plucked their eyebrows to a very thin line. The horns were sometimes so wide that it was difficult for the wearer to get through a doorway.

The heart-shaped head-dress which appeared later in the fifteenth century was

14 The horns on head-dresses gradually became higher and were eventually replaced by the steeple worn by the two ladies on the right.

even more extreme, although it was really a development of the horned. The two "horns" were gradually moved downwards, so that they spread straight out on either side of the head. Veils were attached to the horns and the hair was scooped up into nets on either side of the face. Gradually, the custom developed of wearing an artificial pad or roll on the top of the head and the horns were abandoned. The roll, made of richly embroidered material, formed a heart-shape over the forehead. It was also called the sugar loaf. This head-dress is still worn by the nuns at a convent in Beaune in France.

Probably the most attractive head-dresses were the hennin and the butterfly which appeared towards the end of the century. The hennin, which originated in France, was a cone fixed to a piece of velvet which hung around the face. A piece of net hung from the end of the cone which must have been very difficult to balance on the head. The butterfly was really the English version of the hennin. The cone was cut short, rather like a pudding basin, with pieces of wire sticking out behind, to which veils were attached.

Young girls still wore their hair loose, but for everyone else these extravagant head-dresses meant total concealment of the hair.

Men of the period had reverted to bobbed hair, with a fringe and centre parting, and they shaved the back of the head as they had done in Norman times.

In the fourteenth century barbers and surgeons were organized into two separate City Guilds, which existed to train apprentices and to protect the interests of the members. In those days, barbers not only cut hair but also performed minor surgical operations. This brought them into conflict with the surgeons, who were usually better educated men. There were many quarrels between the two Guilds. In 1540 they were amalgamated by Henry VIII into the Mystery and Commonalty of the Barber-Surgeons' Company. Elizabeth I gave them a crest in 1569; Charles II gave them a loving cup; and Queen Anne a punch bowl. It was not until 1745 that it was recognized that the two professions were somewhat different and they were separated into two companies.

15 At the end of the fifteenth century it was fashionable to shave the forehead, probably the only time in history when apparent baldness has seemed beautiful.

Barbers were then exempt from parish duties and military service which suggests that considerable importance was attached to their trade.

By the end of the Middle Ages, royal families and the aristocracy had become far more firmly established than they had been at the beginning. These settled communities in each country began to accumulate wealth and the king and his court had an increasing influence and power over the lives of the citizens, plus the leisure and money to spend on fashion.

16 In mediaeval times barbers not only cut hair but were also empowered to perform minor operations.

4
The Sixteenth Century and the Renaissance

Hair-styles in the sixteenth century reflect the amazing changes which occurred in society during that era. Everything seemed to be increasing — knowledge, wealth, inventions, exploration, culture, small towns which had once been villages, a few large towns increasing in size to become cities and, most important, the population.

While the king and his court retained their power, and the aristocracy most of the country's wealth, there was among that growing population an increasing number of prosperous citizens. International trade was expanding and Britain's export and import trade led to a new wealthy class of tradesmen who had the money to buy the latest fashions even if they did not have the artistic skill to invent them. The expanding professional classes also felt that one of the best ways of ensuring personal progress was to imitate the aristocracy.

The century began with fashions which still looked mediaeval. It ended with both hair-styles and head-dresses which look attractive even today.

17 The hood became very popular with women at the beginning of the sixteenth century.

18   The ladies in this picture of Sir Thomas
More's family are all wearing the gable, which made
the face look like a framed picture.

At first the hood was worn, draped
around the face and hanging down on the
shoulders and over the back. This meant that
once again the hair was concealed.

The hood gives women a demure look,
like nuns, and suits most faces, which
explains why it was popular for so many
years. As the century progressed, the hood
developed into a gable, stiffened on the
crown of the head to give it shape, with a
pointed arch in front, rising above the forehead. It made every woman's face look like a
picture in a frame. The hair was concealed
under the gable, which was made of metal

or wire, and decorated with jewels or embroidery. The back of the hood, made of silk
and velvet, hung down the back. As time
passed, the pieces of hood hanging down on
either side were also stiffened and covered
with embroidery, so that the face looked
even more like a framed picture.

A new kind of hood imported from
France gradually replaced the gable. It was
the necessary intermediary between the
gable and the new Elizabethan styles which
followed it. Basically, it was a smooth-fitting
cap on the back of the head, from which
hung a hood. The raised front of the cap,
circling the head to the ears, was made of
stiffened velvet or lace, leaving the neck uncovered. Many years later it had developed
into the cap associated with Mary Queen of

Scots. The hair was straight and parted in the centre and fitted smoothly under the cap. But at least, for the first time for years, the hair was actually showing again.

This fact inevitably led women to start experimenting with hair-styles. Queen Elizabeth also contributed to this new interest. She was a redhead (to some extent with the aid of colourants) and she was very proud of her hair, so that auburn, the royal colour, and also blonde were the most fashionable colours for hair. Women at this time dyed their hair with honey or saffron.

When this new phase of styles began, the hair was lightly waved, or rolled back from

19 Mary of Scotland, wearing the smooth cap with a hood at the back, a style which originated in France.

20 This head-dress, worn in the middle of the sixteenth century, combined the best features of the gable and the barbette to create an attractive frame for the face.

the forehead and pinned neatly around the face.

Then the front hair was cut short and dressed in tiny curls around the face. The head-dress during these years became a part of the hair-style: instead of hiding the hair completely, it was used to show off the rolls and curls.

Towards the end of the century this was further enhanced by new fashions, which included a high collar or ruff round the neck. Dresses usually had a fairly low neckline with a ruff attached, encircling the whole neck. The ruff was made of lace or embroidered material and wired to stand up around the head. Sometimes the material

23

was starched to make it stiff. The ruff is probably one of the most flattering styles for a woman and once again her face became a framed picture, but this time encompassed by delicate and jewelled lace.

In fact, the head-dress became merely an added adornment to the hair: pads and wires were worn under the hair so that it could be swept up and arranged in a heart-shape over the forehead. The wire frame grew higher during the last years of the sixteenth century, assuming an oval shape. The hair was swept up over this and held in place with a band of velvet, covered with pearls and jewels. Sometimes the long hair was plaited and wrapped up in a knot on the crown of the head.

Curly hair, with crimped waves and ringlets, was very popular and jewels and coloured stones and ornaments were fixed to the hair with wire. These styles were international and can be seen in many paintings of the time. In the sixteenth century many Italian painters liked painting head-dresses

22   The short neat hair-styles worn by Elizabethan men.

21   Queen Elizabeth I was very interested in fashion. She had hundreds of wigs of different colours, though red was her favourite. Wigs and hair were curled and decorated with jewels. The high collar was also very popular.

and they have recorded many examples of the delicate nets, jewels and braids which were so popular.

In about 1570 wigs were brought over to England from the Continent. Queen Elizabeth I was so enthusiastic about them that a new fashion was created. Often the wigs were used not to cover the hair but were intertwined with it so that there was plenty of hair to be curled and decorated with jewels.

The Queen had hundreds of wigs, and women who could afford to do so bought wigs made from the hair of blonde or red-headed children, or used animal hair if they could not.

At last, women began to go out with no head covering, but perhaps with one or two jewels in their hair for decoration. Young girls had often gone bare-headed but now women did so too. Even the more old-fashioned women who continued to wear hoods had their hair rolled and showing at the sides.

Because the head-dress was no longer part of the hair-style, women started to wear hats instead, which could simply be put on top. They were of all different shapes and sizes, made of a variety of materials, but many of them looked very masculine and did not really go with the feminine hair-styles beneath.

The progress of male hair-styles during the sixteenth century seems to have been in the opposite direction to the development of women's. At the beginning of the century, men's hair was worn long, straight and flowing, whereas even if women did not have their hair cut short, they plaited it. But, from the middle of the century, as women's hair became longer, the fashion for men gradually changed to short hair, which lasted almost to the end of the century. In the 1570s it was brushed up and back.

Perhaps it was natural that men during this century should pay less attention to hair-styles. On the whole, the hero of this age was the explorer and soldier. The brave cavalier was to be admired. Sports like hunting and shooting were the hobbies of the court and of the rich. Searching for new continents and sailing across unknown seas leave no room for personal vanities.

This was an era which ended with Elizabeth's death and the century which followed was to be very different.

23 Boys, like the youthful James I, had very short hair like their fathers, even though the clothes were more elaborate.

25

5
The Seventeenth Century

Until the seventeenth century, the struggle for power had been mainly between the king and the aristocracy. Only a minor part of the population had been involved, sometimes aided and sometimes limited by the Church. But now a new power struggle began between the wealthy and a politically minded middle class, which had not been seen on such a large scale in Britain before. While other European countries have suffered many violent revolutions, the civil war leading to Cromwell's Republic is the only example in English history of a political situation culminating in a revolution.

Strangely enough, the hair-styles of the period seem to exemplify the changing values and ambitions of this turbulent century. They are symbolic, even more than the clothes, of the attitudes and beliefs of their wearers.

The hair-styles of the first half of the century are typical of a wealthy, pleasure-loving elite with time and money to spare. They match the colourful clothes and expensive fabrics. It is a period of curls and ringlets and, although for the first twenty years hair became shorter, it was still dressed in a variety of curls and frizzes.

In the 1630s women started to wear curls on either side of their head, and often they also had a fringe. The ringlets looked very artificial hanging like sausages in neat rows on each side of the face. Jewels in the hair

24 In the reign of Charles I, courtiers wore colourful clothes and long hair with many curls, bows and ringlets.

became less popular, but ribbons and lace were used instead and even feathers.

There was no parting in the hair, which was combed flatly to the back of the head.

Curls were just as popular with men, who had short curls all over their head until about 1630, when long flowing locks, often tied at the end with a ribbon, became more popular.

They also wore a love-lock, a style introduced by James I at the beginning of the century. It was a long curl, hanging down on the left side of the face and often made of false hair.

In fact, men spent as much time and money on their hair as women did, and this provoked much criticism, particularly from the Church. One Puritan writer, William Prynne, wrote in 1628 about "The Unloveliness of Lovelockes":

Infinite and many are the sinfully strange and monstrous Vanities which this Inconstant, Vaine, Fantastique, Idle, Proud, Effeminate and Wanton Age of ours hath Hatched and Produced in all parts and corners of the world . . . .

I have resolved for the present to single out one sinful, shamefull and uncomely vanitie, with which to grapple; which hath lately feigned on many effeminate, loose, licentious, singular, fantastique and vaine-glorious persons, of our masculine and more noble sex; to wit, the nourishing and wearing of unnaturally shamefull and un-lovely Lockes, or Love-Lockes (as they stile them), these lovelockes had their birth from the very Devill himself.

He went on to say that even if people objected that it was only false hair and not their own which they were curling, "the wearing of counterfeite, false and supposititious Haire is *utterly* unlawfull . . .". He also condemned "altering, colouring, crisping or adorning of their heads, wreathings and powdrings".

During the reign of Charles I the developing political struggle, led by Cromwell, brought about a great change in masculine hair-styles.

25 Puritans and Cavaliers could easily be recognized by their clothes and hair-styles, like the Mods and Rockers of recent times.

28

The Puritans, who were opposed to the king, disapproved of all vanity and frivolity. The plainness of their clothes was matched by the plainness of their hair, which was cut short and straight with a fringe. For that reason, these Puritan supporters of Cromwell were called the Roundheads.

The Royalists, on the other hand, believed in the pleasures of court life, which was symbolized for them by their extravagant curls and ringlets.

Hair-styles Post-Cromwell

After the brief ten years of Cromwell's republic (1648-58), hair-styles returned to their previous extravagance.

Women added false curls to their own hair and during the reign of Charles II women wore an even longer curl, called a heart-breaker, which hung down the side of the face. This was a ringlet reaching down to the neck.

In the middle of the seventeenth century Louis XIV of France started a revolution in hair-styles by wearing a wig instead of growing his hair long as so many previous French kings had done. This fashion was introduced into England by Charles II, who had lived on the Continent during his exile.

Wigs for men became very popular. During the sixteenth century the wig had merely simulated real hair and was usually woven in with it, so that you could not tell which was which, or used to conceal baldness. But now wigs became an attraction in their own right, and the real hair was cut very short or shaved off as in Egyptian times.

Often the wigs were powdered in different colours. They were frizzed and curled, with a centre parting and curled horizontally. They were very long, falling to the shoulders and halfway down the back, and there was a

◄ 26　The Puritan influence forced the wives of Cromwell's supporters to wear simple hair-styles and cover their heads.

27　Hair-styles became even more extravagant among fashionable men after the Restoration than they had been before. Wigs became the hall-mark of royalty and men about town.

greater variety than ever before. In fact, no gentleman would be seen without a wig for nearly a century.

Not only courtiers and squires, but professional men also started to wear wigs. Doctors wore wigs "for gravity and importance" and barristers and judges wore a full-bottomed wig (thicker at the bottom), like the French. Before this, judges had worn a velvet cap or one made of white lawn or silk. Now they still put on the black cap to pronounce the death sentence, but it was placed on top of the wig. This custom continued for many years but, by the nineteenth century, the black cap had become a small black spot in the centre of a circular piece of white material placed on the middle of the wig. Even soldiers wore wigs, the long curls of which were tied back with ribbon.

By the end of the seventeenth century, the wigs were so thick and curly that it was impossible to wear a hat, which had to be carried.

Wigs were so popular that a country

28 and 29 Curls and ringlets became popular among ladies in Louis XIV's court in France, and their fashions had a great influence in other European countries.

squire had the Vandyke paintings of his ancestors "improved" by a contemporary artist, by adding wigs to the portraits.

Women were also influenced by the French court. In the second half of the century, wigs became fashionable again for women and hair pieces were used to supplement the wearer's own hair. Dyeing became common, with blonde hair being favoured, although black was popular by the end of the century. Vegetable and flower oils were used for dyeing.

Curls and ringlets were still worn by women and each type of curl had its own name. You could have curls all over the head, rolls of curls down the sides, ringlets on the shoulders — but all were rigidly set in place. One style, called the "scatterbrain", was simply a mass of curls all over the head but even these were securely set in place.

Curling irons were used to set the hair and even at that time there was setting lotion, which was made of glue.

Gradually, the curls on the forehead began to be dressed higher and higher, and this led to a style based on the fontange. The style began when women tied a bow on top of the head and raised the curls above it.

COIFFURE NINON DE L'ENCLOS.

COIFFURE MADAME DE SEVIGNE.

Then, instead of the bow, muslin and lace were mounted on a kind of wire crown with the curls rising around it. A lace or muslin cap kept it on the head. The fontange became so elaborate that it must have been difficult to keep it balanced on the head, although it was popular for about thirty years. It reached its most extreme heights in France. The Fontange was named after Mlle de Fontanges, a mistress of Louis XIV, but there were many other incredible hair-styles and head-dresses. It is only surprising that they continued to be popular for so many years.

The Church maintained its criticism throughout the century. While men were reproved for having long hair, women were criticized if they had theirs cut off. The Bishop of Lincoln wrote a book in 1688 entitled:

Spiritual Armour
To Defend the Head
from the
Superfluity of Naughtiness
Wherein is proved
that it is unlawful for Women to cut their
Hair polled or shorn; and Men to wear the
same to cover their Heads:

The Bishop condemned men for allowing their own locks to grow long or for wearing the locks of women in periwigs. God, he proclaimed, gave women long hair to distinguish them from men! It was women's glory.

30 Later in Louis XIV's reign, a new style was made popular by the Duchess of Fontanges. Muslin and lace were supported by wire above the crown of the head and the hair was curled in ringlets around the face.

6
Eighteenth-Century Extremes

In the early years of the eighteenth century an inevitable reaction set in against the ornate head-gear, and the fontange disappeared. This had been not so much a hair-style as an elaborate head-dress decorated with hair, and the styles which followed were much simpler. Although curls were still worn, most women merely combed their

31 After the fontange (picture 30), hair-styles became simple for a few years. A few ringlets were worn, but no elaborate head-dresses.

COIFFURE MADAME DUBARRY.

hair neatly back from the face in a bun, with a few curls on top.

A popular style was to have the hair combed back with a centre parting and a few ringlets at the back. The lace, net and ribbons and all the other jewelled decorations disappeared, apart from a few pearls which were sometimes used. As the neckline of dresses was low and unadorned, the whole effect was very attractive and this was probably the simplest hair-style in English history. Even colouring the hair became unfashionable.

The eighteenth century was, in fact, rather a sober period in English history. The German kings who now ruled had none of the flamboyance of the Stuarts and fashion became formal and rather dull. Yet, by contrast, for a few years in the middle of the century, women wore one of the most extravagant and even ridiculous hair-styles in European history.

They began to pad the front hair with wool, to raise it higher above their foreheads in the style known as the Pompadour, after Madame de Pompadour, the mistress of Louis XV, who originated it. They then added long horizontal curls at the side and back. Not content with this, they added decorations to the padded hair in front, surmounting it with pearls, ribbons and feathers. Wigs were re-introduced, mixed with real hair, so that the Pompadour in front grew

32 In the eighteenth century English women copied many French hair-styles. A society lady, Mrs John Mortlock, has her hair in the Pompadour style.

33 Mary Isabella, Duchess of Rutland, 1781. Another variation of the Pompadour hair-style, which contrasted with the incredible hair-styles worn at this time.

even higher, and long, thick ringlets developed at the back.

With all the wigs and padding, it was possible to devise many remarkable styles. The padded hair became the base for all kinds of panoramic scenes. Hannah More, a religious writer of the eighteenth century, commented in 1777 that women's hair-styles represented "an acre and a half of shrubbery besides slopes, garden plots, tulip beds, clumps of peonies, kitchen gardens and greenhouses".

In the 1770s a Siberian hair-dresser in London advertised that he "engaged to make any lady's head appear like the head of a lion, wolf, tiger, bear, fox, peacock, swan, goose, Friesland hen or any other bird". Even ostriches could be accommodated.

It was objected that people could not see at the theatre because of ladies' hair, which was surmounted by real flowers and fruit, or models of trees, ships and gardens. The flowers and fruit were sometimes made of hair.

Another very popular style was the hedgehog or poodle. The hair was frizzed in a myriad of tight little curls and scraped back in a huge ball to look just like a hedgehog, or raised upward 30 to 60 centimetres and decorated with flowers and ribbons or anything else that might take women's fancy.

The time and effort taken to achieve these effects were considerable. The hair-style itself with all its padding and curls might

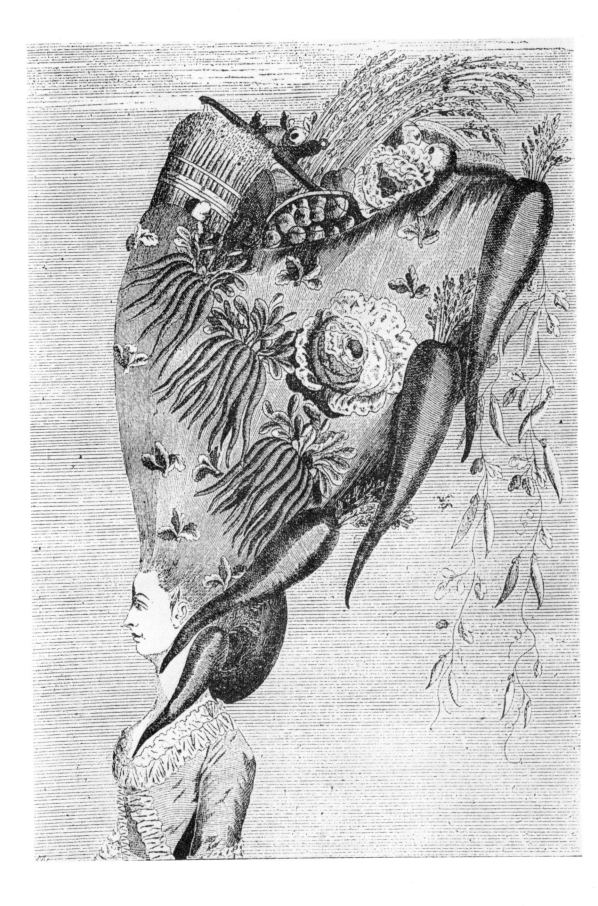

35 The hair was built on a frame which was later removed.

take over 600 curling papers which had to be fitted into a woman's hair. Curling irons heated in the fire were then used to frizz the hair. It was plastered with grease and fitted into position with hundreds of black pins. Perfume was then sprayed over the hair to hide the smell of the grease. To hold the hair in place, it was also possible to have a cap fitted from 50 centimetres to 1 metre in height, "composed of elastic springs which gave way when a lady went into her coach, but rose immediately when she got out again".

The hair-style alone took two or three hours to complete and, as the head-dress grew more elaborate, it became impossible to comb the hair at all. One hairdresser advised that it should be combed only once

34 Women's hair-styles and head-dresses reached incredible proportions. This hair-style is meant to represent a garden.

in eight or ten weeks. When the wearer went to bed, only the head-dress was removed, and the hair was left as it was, with rollers inserted in the curls, to keep them in position, and a lace or muslin cap was added to contain the grease. Some women found it impossible to go to bed at all and slept in chairs, sitting upright.

Special head-scratchers were manufactured, to alleviate the irritation of matted hair and clotted powder.

There was, of course, much criticism of all these excesses and an increasing number of books were written, dealing with the care of the hair. In an article on baldness one writer comments:

Whatever the matter that produces hair, it seems women retain it longer than men; for though we see many men bald, hardly one woman is so without some violent cause; some by pinning hair to the top of the head through the skin; and so fretting and destroying the roots of the hair, by which means the skin becomes bare or by

COIFFURE LA FRÉGATE LA JUNON.

36 This hair-style was thought to be particularly elegant. When going to bed, the wearer would have removed the ship but left the hair as it was!

straining the hair back from the forehead, in moving the eyebrows, in time, will fret away the hair at the edge of the forehead.

This gives some indication of the way in which the hair-styles were held in place!

The same writer also gave warnings about the dangers of some hair-dyeing liquids, "some of which I know will even dye marble of some thickness . . .". But he had an answer: an extract of herbs was recommended:

It is made up in bottles and sold at half a crown each, sealed with my name, with proper directions how to use it.

It was not until the 1780s that some kind of normalcy returned. The absurd headdresses were gradually abandoned and by the 1790s had gone altogether. The great raised

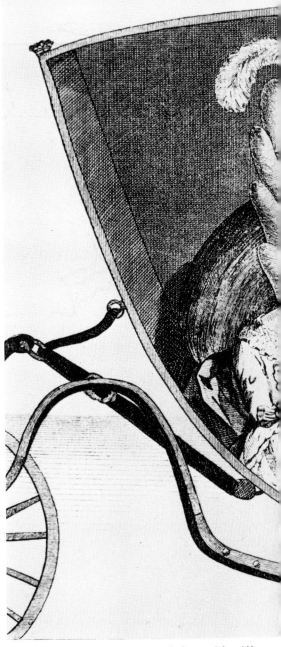

37 These ladies must have ended up with stiff necks if their coach journey took very long!

front of the hair was now turned into a mass of curls with ringlets down the back. Although the hair was set, it was given a more casual and relaxed appearance, with a band

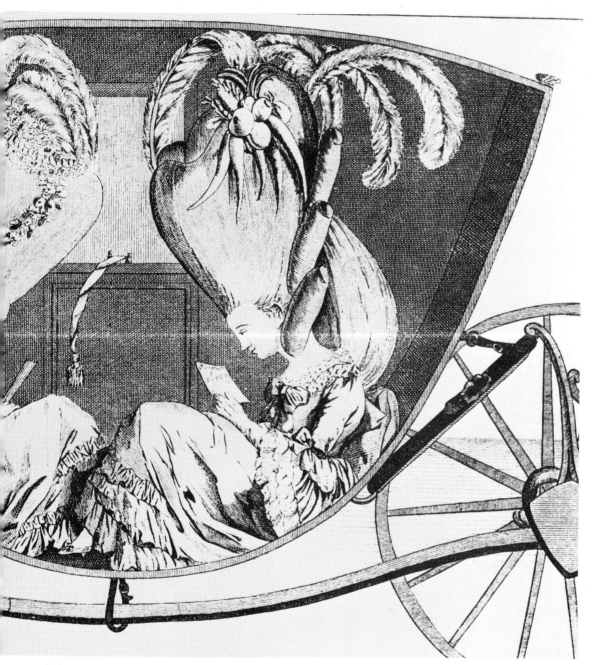

round the head to keep the curls in place.

During the eighteenth century men wore wigs and toupees. A toupee in those days meant the front part of the hair-style, with one or two curls at each ear, and this front hair was curled with hot irons, twisted, made in "scalloped or shelled curls" and powdered. As the favoured colour at that time was white, the hair was powdered with starch. The toupees were often false hair, composed of curls sewn on a ribbon. It was recommended that the hair should be taken down, combed and pinned up again at least once a week, to prevent dandruff.

Full-bottomed wigs remained popular for men during the first half of the eighteenth century but gradually the long, rather thick wig became smaller and the popular style which continued until 1780 was to have rolled curls on either side and a ribbon or bow tied at the back. The blonde and red wigs of the earlier years of the century were gradually replaced in favour of grey.

In spite of the continuing fashion for wigs and false hair, it was no longer usual to cut off one's own hair or to shave the head, though many young men still liked to do so. Lord Chesterfield wrote to his son in 1748:

I can by no means agree to your cutting off your hair. I am very sure that your head-aches cannot proceed from thence.

Of course, financial considerations may have influenced Lord Chesterfield's judgment. Wigs could cost from thirty to forty guineas (about £31 to £42), which was a lot of money in those days.

39 Full-bottomed wigs were worn by men in the services, particularly in the first half of the eighteenth century. The picture shows a French Marshal and subaltern.

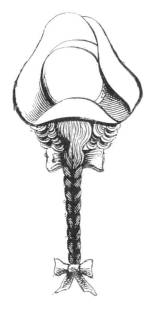

38 For most of the eighteenth century, wigs were worn by men. This one was called the Ramillies wig, named after the Battle of Ramillies of 1706.

By the 1790s wigs had become unfashionable and by the end of the century they were hardly worn, except by lawyers and judges in court and by doctors in their surgeries.

Instead, some men began to have their own hair dressed, and usually powdered. But during the Napoleonic wars it became much more expensive to use powder and the Prime Minister, William Pitt, imposed a heavy tax on it. Fashionable men were outraged, and many pamphlets attacked this new tax, including one written by Brutus — "Cursory

40 Examples of the wigs and toupees worn by ▶ men in the eighteenth century.

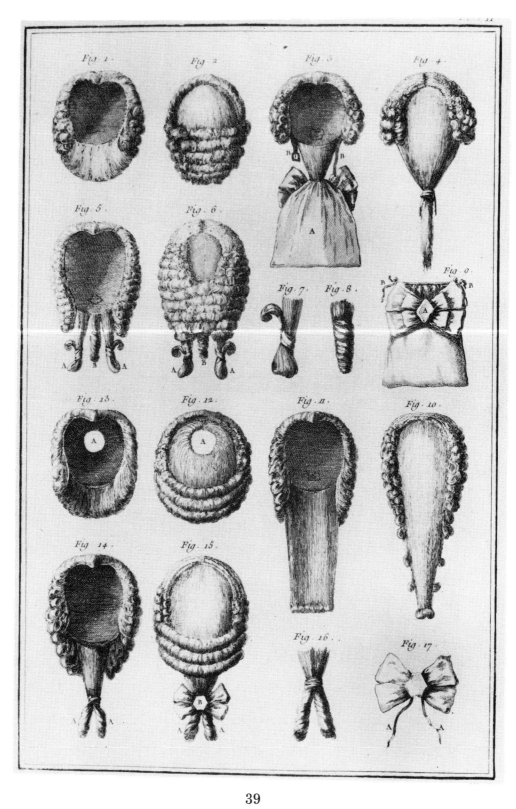

41 Throughout the eighteenth century, barbers continued to do a flourishing trade in wigs. The picture shows (a) barber shaving someone's beard, (b) arranging a wig, (c) and (d) making wigs, (e) heating curling tongs, (f) gentleman wiping powder from his face.

Remarks on Mr Pitt's New Tax of Imposing a Guinea per head on every person who wears hair-powder":

We have contented and entertained our-selves with laughing at and sporting our jokes at the ludicrousness of the subject; but we have not condescended to reflect on its impolicy, its absurdity, its injustice and the oppression it must necessarily inflict.

And yet the people of England, the people of a free country, that are inces-santly boasting of their glorious Constitu-tion are to be dragooned by the authority of an Act of Parliament, being told that we are paying for our Pride and Vanity!

All luxuries ought to be taxed. Why not tax keeping hounds, shooting, keeping carriages?

And all, as he adds, "to support a war which will be our ruin".

For the men who were now abandoning wigs, Brutus gave detailed instructions on setting the hair in the most fashionable style, which was a combination of real and false hair, ribbons and silk:

Tie hair close to the neck, the remainder to be put up, smooth or plaited and wrapt round with a black ribbon or enclosed in a full-dress silk bag.

The top of the head may be curled in the shape of a horseshoe or frizzed back from the forehead, rising highest in the middle — this style is called Allegreek. Side curls are layered in one to three rows, one above the other. The hair must be powdered.

40

42 Hair-styles common just before the Revolution, French (left) and English (centre and right).

Allegreek was a style recommended for use with hats, though it must have been difficult to wear a hat behind the horseshoe.

The partly bald were recommended to wear "towers", which were half-wigs, and many men wore their own hair and simply added false long hair for the back.

In the latter part of the eighteenth century men were still wearing the queue — the long hair, tied with a large bow or ribbon at the back and, of course, powdered.

The French Revolution had a great effect on hair-styles, as it had on many other aspects of social life. The starving citizens of the Paris communes would not have been likely to approve of the extravagant head-dresses of the 1770s and there was an inevitable trend towards natural hair-styles — even

if they were only set to *look* natural. Clothes became simpler and hair-styles followed.

A male fashion arose in France for long, straight, untidy hair, looking straggly and uncombed, presumably in imitation of the triumphant if dishevelled citizens. The men who followed this fashion were called Incroyable and were instantly followed by a female counterpart, Merveilleuse. Whether they were supporting the revolutionaries or mocking them, or were hoping to disguise themselves, is difficult to say.

An even more bizarre hair-style was that based on the appearance of the victims of the revolution. Hair-styles known as "à la guillotine" and other suitable epithets had the hair cropped short all round and usually straight. This was in imitation of the unfortunate aristocrats who had had their long curls shorn off in the prison cells before going to the guillotine.

However, most women wore their hair drawn back in a simple bun or tied neatly with a bandeau or with a coil of hair. This was based on what was believed to be the early Greek hair-style, although it was only a pale imitation.

The extravagance of the Versailles court, always more extreme than that of the English court, was never seen again. But although there was this temporary period of simplicity during the French Revolution, hair-styles were to go through as many changes in the next century as they had done in all others, some simple, some more sophisticated. The introduction of new materials also influenced the hair-styles which would go under caps, hats and hoods.

43 Styles seen during the Revolution years. Did they hope to look like the citizens or were they mocking them?

7
Victorian England

The nineteenth century was dominated by Queen Victoria and many of the fashions and attitudes emanated from her.

For the first thirty-seven years, before she came to the throne, women's hair remained short, but the simple style gradually developed into more and more curls. False curls and hair pieces were mixed with real hair and a few beads or pearls were added for decoration. The styles were remarkable not so much because of the curls and ringlets as for the angles at which these were worn. Curls were massed on the forehead and ringlets or curls hanging on either side of the face were tied tightly with ribbons so that they stuck out like horns at the side of the head, or they were tied firmly on top of the head. The intention was to achieve a sickly sort of prettiness, so that women's heads looked rather like presents tied up with ribbons and bows. These styles grew higher and higher, with hair in coils and braids, and a fashion developed for imitating the ringlets seen in many seventeenth-century portraits.

Black hair was fashionable at this time and women's magazines devoted much space to advising women about dyeing their hair.

When Victoria appeared, a new era began. At the beginning of her reign the young queen favoured youthful simplicity and this was instantly copied by many fashion-conscious women who are always greatly influenced by royal example. The forehead curls vanished and the hair was completely flat on top, although curls or ringlets were occasionally worn at the sides. At her coronation, Victoria's hair was parted in the middle with the ends plaited over the ears and curved upwards. The back hair was divided, plaited and wound round at the

44 A curious style of the early 1900s, worn by the Princess Lieven. Hair was tied tightly with ribbons on either side of the head, so that it stuck out like horns.

COIFFURE "1830," by **CROISAT.**

45 The styles grew higher and more elaborate. Dyeing became popular, with bows, combs and ribbons for decoration.

back. This style continued for some years, with variations of a bun or chignon at the back.

As we have seen, hair-styles and head-dresses have always had symbolic meanings, from the Gods-worship of the Egyptians to the simplicity of the Roundheads. The Victorians were great image-builders of the domestic scene. Their hair fashions represented the demure respectability which was imposed by newly-rich men on their wives, who were treated as personal possessions.

46 The hair-style worn by Victoria at her coronation. She influenced women to wear their hair in plain and simple styles.

47 Variations of the Victorian style. Buns and chignons were meant to make women look demure and respectable.

The industrial revolution helped to create a growing number of middle-class women whose husbands provided them with a home and servants so that they had very little to do. They were expected only to make themselves a living proof of their husband's prosperity, which is one of the reasons why the Victorian home became the repository of every kind of handicraft, both useful and otherwise.

By the end of the century, when the queen's age and isolation meant that she had

little effect on fashion, hair-styles gradually became more extreme. However, for most of her long reign, they remained subdued and rather unattractive.

Indoor caps, made of muslin, lace, ribbon or silk flowers, also became an absolute necessity for the Victorian lady and these demanded a simple and demure hair-style. Sometimes a fillet was worn, covering the ears, but as the years passed, caps became more and more frilly and lacy, making the Victorian matron look like an overgrown Alice in Wonderland.

During the 1840s and 50s the hair was generally parted in the centre and combed smoothly down, ending in ringlets on either side of the face. In a booklet on *How to Arrange the Hair*, written by one of the Ladies Committee of Almacks (a fashionable London club) in 1857, it is noted that "hair has been for a long period worn Madonna-like, drawn plain over each cheek, like the Queen".

Early in the 1860s styles became more varied, with more ringlets and rolls again.

48 At the end of the century buns and curls had become a little more elaborate. This style was called the "Jug handle".

Hair was gradually dressed more and more at the back with rolls and curls, plaits or a chignon, sometimes with five rolls intertwined. There might be a few curls on the top of the head but none at the sides.

Sometimes false hair, about a metre in length, was intertwined with the real hair to make the chignon large at the back. It was kept in place with ribbons or nets held down with beads. It was impossible to wear a hat with this style, so the rolls of hair were decorated instead with tortoise-shell combs, plaits, roses and trailing flowers.

Towards the end of the century, the chignon was abandoned but the false curls, bun or top knot continued.

Hair was swept up at the sides, looking full and smooth, and the image of the dignified lady took the place of Alice in Wonderland.

Large gilt pins with balloon-like tops were used to keep the high styles in place and shell beads and combs with gold-beaded edging were popular. Feathers and ostrich plumes were also used for decoration.

Although Queen Victoria tolerated the wearing of white plumes, she thought that coloured plumes were too showy for her court. In 1879 she ordered that all plumes had to be worn so that they could be clearly seen, in order to ensure that no forbidden coloured plumes were concealed amongst the curls. (This is reminiscent of the autocratic rules at Wimbledon in the twentieth century, which laid down that competitors should wear only white.)

In the 1880s a thick fringe of curls became popular with tight curls all round. This required a short hair-cut, and once again Victoria forbade the wearing of short hair at court, so that anyone adopting the new hair-style had to attach false curls or ringlets if they wished to be admitted.

Dyeing the hair became popular again and instructions were given in many ladies' journals and magazines. These periodicals for the new leisured class had proliferated along with the great increase in the number of domestic servants, encouraging their readers to occupy their time on personal adornment.

For darkening grey hair, a mixture of acetate of lead, sulphur, balsam, beef marrow and castor oil was recommended. In the 1870s golden hair became popular and this was achieved with powder or by bleaching with peroxide, which had been discovered by a Frenchman in 1818. There was also a craze for red hair as there had been in Elizabethan times.

For setting hair, carbonate of potassium, ammonia, glycerine, spirit and rose water were mixed into a solution which was then poured on the hair.

Magazines also gave detailed information about creating each individual hair-style.

A remedy for falling hair was petrol mixed with a few drops of perfume, while the hair "should be fixed in place with white wax, pure lard and perfume", presumably the fore-runner of setting lotion.

Another curious occupation of the Victorian lady was making keep-sakes of real hair. The many knick-knacks, crafts, needlework and crocheted objects which cluttered the Victorian home were really the result of the ladies' boredom. Anything that could occupy their minds for a few hours was welcome, and the whole century is filled with the various "manias" from foreign countries which they adopted for brief periods. Embroidering hair pictures was one of them, brought back from Siberia, and adapted to their own materials and capabilities.

It began through the practice of keeping a lock of hair of a friend or loved one. This was kept in a locket or frame, but later it began to be made into some "little device". Instructions were given in *The Lock of Hair* about how to deal with it. It took many pages to explain how to clean the lock of

49 Men had beards and moustaches, but wigs ➤ were out of fashion. Both men and women had centre partings. The curly fringe became popular towards the end of the century. The picture shows the Morris and Burne-Jones families, 1874.

47

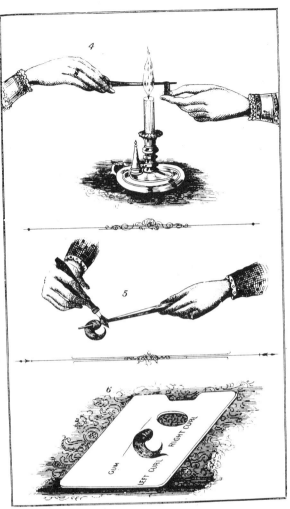

50 An illustration from *The Lock of Hair*, showing idle Victorian ladies how to make hair into a "design".

There was even a portrait of Queen Victoria worked in hair at the Great Exhibition of 1851.

The other abiding passion throughout the century was for false hair which continued to be used for curls, ringlets and plaits. It was justified in *The Lock of Hair* on the grounds that:

as one of the symbols of age, baldness is a defect which every woman, not to say man, is fairly bound to compensate by artificial adornment. Egyptian paintings 6000 years ago exhibit wigs of the most exquisite and ornate character

However, false hair used by Victorians was not mainly for the purpose of hiding baldness.

There was an enormous trade in false hair, which was imported from all over the Continent, particularly blonde hair from Germany and Scandinavia. It was estimated that 91,000 kgs weight of human hair was sold on the Parisian market every year. Poor people and peasant girls were the main suppliers. In France and Germany, pedlars went round the country buying the hair of young girls and women in the villages, who grew it year after year to sell for the market.

It was collected during the spring and summer when it was supposed to be in its best condition and was called the "hair harvest".

The donors kept a small portion of hair in front and, by wearing a hood or head-scarf, could conceal the fact that there was no hair at the back. The hair could never be grown fast enough or in sufficient quantities to satisfy the market. It took about six years for the hair to reach a good commercial length and the donors were paid from 1/- to 5/- (5p to 25p) a pound for their tresses.

Some pedlars offered flashy jewellery instead of money although it was probably worthless. Some hair which was particularly fine and of the current fashionable colour was sold for a great deal more than the

hair, with borax and soda, scrape it, rinse it and then spread it on a palette in order to produce "a well-known and justly-admired design called the Prince of Wales' feather". Even more pages were then devoted to a description of how to use the curling irons, heated with a candle, to curl the hair into the required shape.

The book provides ample proof of the absurdity of the Victorian woman's position, and of the absurd activities she indulged in to pass the time.

donor had been paid. It could cost as much as 60/- (£3) a pound.

Victor Hugo, the nineteenth-century French writer, commented that a poor young girl "parts with her hair, then her two front teeth" which were sold for false teeth for wealthy people.

False hair was often obtained from country districts in England. Thomas Hardy's novel *The Woodlanders*, published in 1876, opens with the visit of a master barber to a country girl to try to persuade her to sell her hair to him:

> *he beheld a girl seated on a willow chair and busily working by the light of the fire . . . . She had but little pretension to beauty except in one prominent particular — her hair.*
>
> *Its abundance made it almost unmanageable; its colour was, roughly speaking, and as seen here by firelight, brown; but careful notice, or an observation by day, would have revealed that its true shade was a rare and beautiful approximation to chestnut.*
>
> *"Here's a sovereign — a gold sovereign, almost new. That's as much as you'd earn in a week and a half . . . and it's yours for just letting me snip off what you've got too much of."*

In orphanages, children's hair was often closely cropped, partly for cleanliness but also for commercial reasons.

During Victoria's reign men's hair-styles became drab and undistinguished, a phase from which they are only now recovering. For most of the century, they wore their hair short, brushed forward in curls, which were worn longer in the 1830s. At that time the hair was elaborately styled, with a centre parting and the hair brushed forward. The styles were also influenced by Victoria's husband, and the German Roll was fashionable for some years. For this style, the hair was cut to a length of 15-18 centimetres, combed neatly and turned under at the ends, reminiscent of Puritan hair-styles in the seventeenth century.

By the 1880s hair was cut short at the back and sides and this became the norm for men for about a century. It was partly the result of living and working in a new industrial society.

Wigs continued to be worn only by male servants of the aristocracy and of the upper classes, but they were shorter and were made of artificial material, not real hair.

51 The domestic servant was expected to dress for the part, to emphasize her master's social importance. Hair-styles were simple, to accommodate the linen cap.

The *Hairdressers' Journal* commented in 1863:

It is believed that the fate of powdered wigs was sealed in this country by George III in consequence of finding a moving evidence of one of their products in his dinner plate, and which was supposed to be the property of one of the royal flunkeys, but which the satirists of the day were inclined to suppose was a wanderer from the royal head itself.

It praised the new and "extraordinary spun glass wigs of the coachmen of the upper ten thousand. They replace the powdered wigs and are infinitely more cleanly".

Hairdressing benefited from the advances of the new industrial age. One of the most important developments was a method of producing natural-looking waves with special curling tongs invented by Marcel. He was born in France in 1852 and by the end of the 1880s the technique was widely practised in this country. It meant that for the first time, women's hair could be lightly waved instead of frizzed, as it had been with the old curling irons.

Waves and rolls gradually replaced curls and ringlets although till the end of the century the smooth, upswept hair with curls or a top knot were still the most common.

Interest in hair-styles was so great that exhibitions began to be held to demonstrate the new techniques. One of the first was held in Hulme Town Hall, Manchester, in December 1874 "to show unusual modes of dressing ladies' hair by twelve experts".

By the end of the century, another new influence was affecting hair-styles. With the growth of cities, the amenities of city life also grew and a visit to the theatre became another popular symbol of middle-class prosperity, giving the ladies an opportunity to display their dresses and jewels. But it also meant that they started to imitate the actresses whom they went to see. This was the fore-runner of the film-star craze of the twentieth century. Pictures of actresses appeared in magazines and young stage-struck Victorian girls copied their clothes and hair-styles.

The sombre Victorian age was almost over.

8
The Modern World

The biggest single factor which has influenced hair and hair-styles and many other aspects of life in the twentieth century has been the increased spending power of women. This spending power was confined in Victorian times to the new middle-class woman, dependent on her husband's success in factory or business. But in the twentieth century it has been extended to women of all classes, who can provide incomes for themselves, whether single or married.

Two world wars, the extension and development of an industrial society towards a technological society, universal education, opportunities for travel, careers for women, all accelerated the liberation of women from Victorian domesticity.

The growing power of women is reflected in the amount of female-orientated advertising today. The increasing numbers of women's magazines not only bear witness to the fact that all women can now partake of the material benefits offered by society, but also reflect the growing independence of women. Increasingly, while making use of the opportunities presented, women conform less and less to any rigid patterns.

At one time, the latest fashion which appeared in shops and hairdressing salons was instantly adopted by all. But in the last few years, there have been instances of new "fashions" being total failures because the female salary earner did not like them. This change is nowhere more apparent than in the attitudes to hair and hair-styles.

The century opened on an Edwardian world still influenced by the Victorians. It began quietly enough, with rather dignified, upswept hair, soft and full and dressed in a Pompadour style. It was puffed out over a pad inserted across the forehead, and the back hair was pulled up and held in place with combs. The style was worn by Edward VII's wife, Queen Alexandra.

Thick, wavy hair was popular and it was now possible to buy a wig — called a transformation — of wavy hair, instead of the previous curls and ringlets. Long hair was plaited and coiled at the back and large-brimmed hats were kept on with long, jewelled hat pins which have since become collectors' items. Many of these hair-styles were rather elegant, although Edwardian women look rather forbidding.

The first great change, perhaps the biggest single event in the history of hairdressing, was the invention of the permanent wave in 1904. It was developed by a German called Charles Nessler, who went to America in 1906. He demonstrated it in London in the same year.

He used solid brass curlers and the perm took a whole day to complete. Initially, it was a very painful process, because the electrically heated curlers were heavy and difficult to keep at the right temperature.

THE 'EVERYDAY" HAIR STYLE

A practical everyday coiffure for young and old, and can be kept with care for two weeks without skilled attention.

This design is very versatile, as it can be dressed to suit practically all types of faces to advantage.

The design shows a backward movement of deep waves with a formation of masses of strong curls above the ears. Have this style dressed upon your new perm.

52 The permanent wave started a new era for women, although at the beginning it could be a painful operation.

Many ladies went home with a scorched head, although they probably felt it was worth it. For the first time, they actually had waves and curls which would last, with little attention, for six months or until the hair grew out. On the other hand, it was very expensive to begin with, and only the wealthy could benefit from the new invention.

At about the same time, however, Marcel began to market curling tongs for use at home. The soft Marcel wave was still very popular and vied with the new permanent wave which, at the beginning, tended to be very tightly waved and curled.

Soft hair-styles were still the most popular, with the hair full and rather wide on each side of the face. It was padded or wound round small wire frames and held in place with combs. Transformations, the wavy wigs, were worn with tortoiseshell combs. This was followed by flatter, lightly waved hair-styles and just before the First World War, bobbed hair was introduced.

During the war years there was little change of fashion. Women, for the first time in uniform or working in factories, still wore dresses reaching almost to their ankles and the short, lightly waved hair, sometimes swept up at the back in a neat chignon or a bun, lasted throughout the war.

When it ended, a new era began. Women were not willing to return to sheltered domesticity and second-class citizenship. The fact that some of them obtained the vote was less important than the fact that many more of them entered the job market. Probably women have never realized how important the increasing use of the type-writer was to their liberation.

The new hair-styles perhaps reflected unconsciously women's entry into the masculine world. In 1918 hair became straight and smooth and the short bob was popular. But in the early 1920s the shingle was introduced, a short straight cut which was even shorter at the back of the head. This was popular for several years, getting shorter and shorter.

53 A combination of the soft Marcel wave and the shingle which appeared in the early 1920s.

54 The Eton crop appeared in 1926 and looked too masculine for many people to accept.

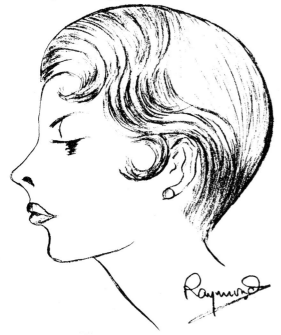

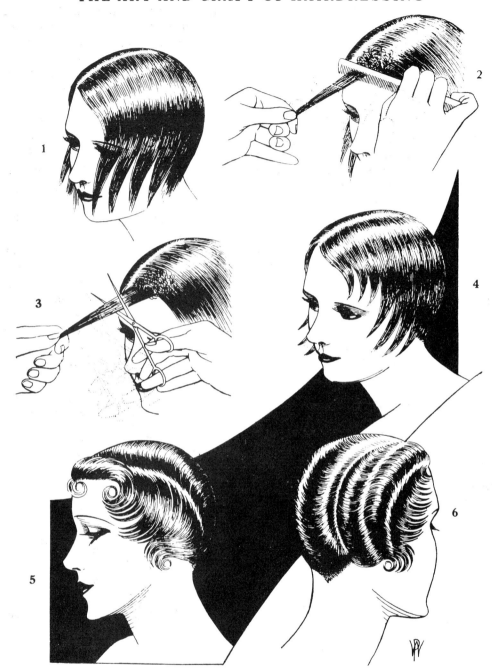

THE "WINDBLOWN" COIFFURE

Fig. 1. Showing Hair Combed Towards Face

Fig. 3. Method of Tapering Sections

Fig. 5. Showing how Hair is Set towards the Face

Fig. 2. Method of Sectioning Hair, and Back-combing

Fig. 4. Showing Series of Varied Lengths on Completion of Taper

Fig. 6. Showing Back and Small Side of Completed Dressing

It aroused violent criticism and abuse in the press. During the war short hair had been looked upon as a sign of patriotism, but short hair for women was now considered to be almost indecent. In the minds of many men, it was synonymous with suffragettes and equal rights.

By the summer of 1925, however, plaits or waves might be seen again and Marcel's Home Outfit encouraged women to wave their hair at home.

It was in the mid-twenties also that, for the first time in history, women began to wear skirts which exposed not only their ankles but also their knees. In November 1926 the *Sunday Mercury* reported that:

A large hospital tried to forbid its nurses to have their hair cut. For fear of reprisals the order seems to have been obeyed. But the hospital found that it could not get replacements and the notices were withdrawn.

The Eton crop, which was introduced in 1926, provoked even more controversy. The hair was cut above the ears and very short at the back, shorter in fact than most men's, although often very long ear-rings were worn to soften the appearance.

There was also a cult for wearing a fringed bob, introduced by a film star called Anna May Wong. Claudette Colbert, another film star, introduced a development of this by curling the fringe in a "bang" and this was widely copied.

Experts predicted that the shingle would last for at least another century and at the beginning of the thirties it was still the most popular style. Various styles developed from it. First, there was the bingle, a shorter version of the shingle. Then came the mingle, a style which included curls and waves mingled in "an artistic manner". The mingle was longer than the shingle, in order to have enough hair to curl.

This led to the Windblown, the Cherub, the Madonna and the Cringle. Although these were cleverly linked by hairdressers with the popular shingle, they were in fact totally different because they were all based on perming and setting. Hairdressers had recognized the importance of cutting and tapering and the hairdressers' magazine, the *Gallia Messenger*, in 1932 discussed the new tapering scissors which had been invented.

These new hair-styles, which originated in France, brought women back to the hairdressing salon. The styles were "eccentric or slightly fantastic" or were advertised as being such. The Windblown was, of course, an artistic simulation of windswept curls, and was meant to look like a girl standing with her back to the wind, hair being blown forward in a wispy manner on to her face. It was recommended that it "should be worn only by women with a suitable physiognomy".

The Cherub had rolls of curls at the neck. The Madonna was parted in the centre with two rows of curls, and the Cringle was set in upward sweeping waves.

In fact, although hair was still short, the "perm" had at last established itself. More and more women went to the hairdresser's and from that time onwards, there was a profusion of new hair-styles.

Water-waving was another system where the waves were pinched into shape before drying. The new hooded dryer meant that hair could more successfully be set into place, because of the even heat over the whole head which had not been possible with the earlier blow dryer.

At the Hairdressing Fair of Fashion at Olympia in 1932 hairdressers were shown the latest methods in perms, water-waving and setting, and there were new soapless shampoos, dyes and conditioners.

An important influence in the 1930s and 40s was that of the film stars. Until after the end of the Second World War, the cinema was the most popular and universal form of entertainment, and the hair-styles of the

◄ 55   Although the cutting looks "windblown", the final set looks anything but that!

shoulder-length hair which has never completely gone out of fashion.

In the late 30s and 40s upswept hair-styles came into fashion, with curls piled on top of the head reminiscent of Edwardian styles.

During the war years hair was once again cut short, partly because of regulation lengths in the women's services. Long hair was dangerous in war-time factories, where large numbers of women were employed.

It was quite usual for hair to be cut to 7.5 centimetres all over the head, upswept at the sides and back, with curls on top. Longer rolling curls were also popular, but were usually swept up, with curled rolls at the back.

With the end of the war, hair tended to be

56 Hollywood had an enormous impact on fashion. In the '30s these hair-styles were thought to be of "particular individuality".

stars were imitated all over the world. Greta Garbo started the trend in 1932, with her simple style of hair combed back behind the ears and curled loosely under at the back. It was basically a bob, but from this developed the page boy, where the hair was much longer and turned under at the ends. This was made popular by another film star in 1937 and continued to be popular all over the world for about ten years.

The snood, a net for enclosing the hair at the back, was also popular at the beginning of the Second World War, as was loose

57 Hairdressing competitions became popular in the '30s. This won the first prize for the Nestlé System of Permanent Waving at Olympia in 1932.

58　A style reminiscent of over a century earlier.
This original coiffure, a representation of a peacock,
was made entirely of human hair.

THe Bouffant
1950

cut. The hair was cut short in irregular lengths all over the head and brushed forward from the crown. It was a charming and rather piquant style.

Home perms were not introduced until about 1948, although they had been mentioned in ladies' journals in the 1900s. By the 1950s they were extensively used and although there was a corresponding increase in the number of women who went to the hairdressers, only 18 per cent of all women went in November 1949, with an average expenditure of £1. 8. 4d.

In 1952, there were over 36,000 hairdressing salons employing about 90,000 people.

The 1950s might be called the decade of the birth of the teenager in Britain. The young woman — and the young man — still living at home, with a regular income, had more money to spend on clothes and hairdressing than ever before, and advertisements in magazines encouraged her to spend her money. Great improvements were made in both tints and dyes and in the techniques for their application, with many new sprays, lacquers and conditioners.

What had been happening to men's hairstyles throughout these fifty years? For most of that time, men's hair was short and neat with a side or centre parting. Wigs had completely disappeared, except to hide baldness, and even beards were rarely seen, except on sailors or intellectuals, although moustaches were common until the First World War. Brilliantines and hair creams were used by almost all men, plastered on the hair to keep it firmly in place. Men did go to the barber's, but for men this was associated only with shaving and hair cuts. However, the attempt to get men into the hairdresser's had already begun through advertising.

59   The Bouffant popular in the 1950s has appeared again in the 1980s, but looking now rather more formal and neat.

grown longer but for a few years there was no really distinctive style.

In the 1950s the beehive, a bouffant hairstyle, with long hair drawn to the top of the head and the hair back-combed, appeared. This was lacquered to keep it in place and was popular throughout the decade.

The pony-tail was also worn with the hair scraped back from the face and fixed at the back with ribbon or combs or even an elastic band.

Another popular style in the 50s was the urchin cut, also called the razor or poodle

60   In the 1930s fashion in men's hair-styles was ➤ set by film stars like George Raft, seen here in *It Had To Happen*, 1936. Men wore their hair short and parted and smoothed down with much brilliantine.

In the 1930s there were various "glamorous" names for men's hair-styles — The Bombage, Bressant, à la Brosse, Convict Crop, and Bushy — but today they all look alike, all short back and sides, all straight, swept back and smoothed down with brilliantine.

A survey in 1949 showed that 80 per cent of all men went to a barber in that November, but of 1,273 men questioned, only 8 had had a shampoo.

The 1960s saw a dramatic change which continues to this day, in relation to both men and women. For women, there has been a firm tendency to wear their hair as they please and in the style that suits them. It would be difficult to pick on any hair-style as being typical. Hair may be long or short, straight, curly or waved, and one can only say that hair-styles tend to be more casual and more adaptable to change.

The art of cutting hair has received much more attention. Tints are popular still and perms tend to be soft and casual. Wigs may or may not be worn, according to inclination, and can be bought in any colour or style or length, with either real or imitation hair. Wigs were worn extensively a few years

62 Modern hair-styles may be anything from long and straight to short and spiky. This stark hair-style is reminiscent of the extremes of the French Revolution.

61 Michael Dahl, self-portrait. It is difficult to believe that this was a hair-style worn in 1691. He belongs just as easily to the twentieth century.

63 A multi-coloured style with a message (the ➤ top hair is coloured like the union jack). But is the style appropriate to the message?

ago but have been superseded at the moment by a great variety of soft perms.

If we look in any woman's magazine, or look at the photos in the hairdressing salons in the High Street, we can see that styles now tend to be modelled around the wearer, as distinct from the past when everyone wore a particular hair-style whether it suited her or not.

For men, the change has been even more dramatic. The short hair of the Teddy Boy era of the 1950s seems to have made men aware once again of hair-styles.

It is interesting that in an age of growing equality, there seems to have been an increasing tendency towards hero-worship. The 1930s and 40s were dominated by the film stars. Millions of photographs issued from

Hollywood, and men and women all over the world imitated their hair-styles.

This was followed by the pop star era, heralded in by the Beatles. Their hair-style, combed forward, still fairly short but distinctively shaped, was followed by millions of youths all over the world.

After nearly a century of short back and sides, hair grew longer and longer and it became increasingly popular for the hair to look as rough and straggly as possible. This

64 The intricately plaited hair-style popular with black girls. Not the sort of thing you could cope with if you overslept and had a train to catch!

phase was shared by young men and women and led to the unisex styles, where it was often difficult to distinguish one sex from the other.

However, they had an enormous influence and long hair was finally worn by all men, young and old alike.

Minority groups, trying to make themselves heard and noticed, find that the hair is a natural way of drawing attention to oneself. The Mods and Rockers and the Flower People all had their own distinctive way of doing their hair. Health foods people and those living a "back to nature" life also seem to favour long, untidy hair and recently we have seen a cult for violent colours — red, green and blue for young men and women, reminiscent of the Anglo-Saxons.

The "skinhead" hair-style and many similar styles seem to be designed to make people look as unattractive as possible. The hair-styles again have a symbolic meaning for the wearers. It is their way of telling polite and respectable society that they are not interested in society's norms, that they are free to cut and colour their hair as they please.

The very long hair for men is no longer fashionable but, like women, men now tend to wear their hair as they wish, although with far fewer styles and variations. Many men now go to the hairdresser's for shampoos, sets, blow waves and tinting as often as their girl-friends.

Another development, to "cure" baldness, has been the transplant, a technique of putting living hair into the scalp. This makes a wig unnecessary and is permanent. When it becomes an economic proposition for more men, it is likely to be very popular.

Ironically, with everyone "doing their own thing", it has been an absolute bonanza for the hairdressers.

65 and **66**   Long hair continues to be a "style for
all seasons", mainly because it gives so much scope
for a variety of styles.

9
Hairdressing as a Career

The opportunities in hairdressing as a career have probably expanded more in the last twenty years than at any time in history.

To a certain extent, this can be attributed to the greatly increased interest in hair-styles taken by men. The Beatles contributed to this new interest. At the time their rather stylised hair cut was revolutionary, although today it looks ordinary enough. But, in contrast with the Teddy Boy styles of the 1950s, it did require expert cutting and styling.

The number of men going to the hairdresser's has increased dramatically and of 47,200 hairdressing salons recorded in the Census of 1971, one third were men's.

Today, about 140,000 people are employed in the hairdressing industry.

There has also been a steady expansion of women's hairdressing. Styles change constantly and women are willing to experiment with different colours, cuts and perms.

There are two recognized methods of entry to the profession. The most usual is to become an apprentice in a hairdressing salon. Every town and village now has a men's and women's hairdresser's, but it is important to check that a proper training will be given.

Every women's hairdresser must now be able to cut, set, use colours and dyes and permanent wave, as well as being able to dress and style wigs and hair-pieces. The hairdresser in the High Street may employ up to half a dozen people, although larger salons in town centres may have more. There is usually a maximum of about ten.

Training begins between 16 and 18 years of age, lasts for three years, and normally apprentices now attend local technical colleges on day-release, in order to take the two stages of the City and Guilds examinations.

The Guild of Hairdressers also offers a more advanced diploma.

Men's salons are run on similar lines, with the emphasis on styling, waving and colouring. The old concept of the barber who simply shaved men's beards and trimmed their hair is disappearing. Many more men now have their hair shampooed. An interesting hangover from the past is that it is still less usual for men to make appointments at the hairdresser's.

At one time, apprentices had to pay a premium to the hairdresser who accepted them for training, but this has almost died out. However, it is still customary to buy your own tools, which will cost up to £20.

The other method of training is to take a two-year full-time course at a College of Further Education where, apart from hairdressing skills, students are taught how to care for equipment, the scientific aspects of hair treatment and dyes, and they must also be able to dress wigs, switches and hair-pieces.

There are also two-year courses and three-year apprenticeships in wig-making. This is an expanding field because as well as the popularity of wigs for fashion, the National Health Service provides wigs for people who need them. Wig-making is a highly skilled job requiring much patience and good eyesight for matching the different shades of hair.

After training, there are various openings for the qualified hairdresser, other than work in the normal salon. There are usually salons in department stores and in many large hotels. There are clubs in many cities with a resident hairdresser, and health clinics and residential clubs have salons. Film and television studios obviously have hairdressers, although there is much competition for these jobs.

In the past, hairdressing was very poorly paid and as a result there is a Wages Council to ensure that wages paid by employers are adequate.

Wages Registration Orders control the minimum wage and cover provision of holidays, and all employers are bound by law to follow these regulations. In addition, commission is generally paid and there is still a long-standing tradition of giving tips at hairdresser's, although this is apparently more common among women than men.

Hairdressing also promises to provide secure employment for many years to come, for it seems that we shall never lose interest in hair and hair-styles.

Glossary

Afro	Frizzed hair-style like natural African hair.
à la guillotine	Short hair-style seen during French Revolution.
Allegreek	A male hair-style of the eighteenth century.
back comb	A method of making hair full by holding strands of hair upwards and combing from the ends towards the roots. Popular in the 1960s.
bag wig	Hair tied at back and enclosed in a black silk bag with a draw string. Worn by men, mid-eighteenth century.
bang	A roll of hair or fringe over forehead, twentieth century.
barbette	Flat chin-strap attached to each side of fillet, fourteenth century.
beehive	A bouffant hair-style, with hair puffed out and drawn to top of head, twentieth century.
bingle	Shorter version of the shingle, 1930s.
bob	Very short hair, usually just level with ears, 1920s.
bun	Hair, usually straight, pinned at back of head in a bun shape.
butterfly	Truncated cone cap with light veiling erected by means of wires, fifteenth century. It was the English version of the hennin.
Cherub	Short hair-style with rolls of curls at the neck, 1920s.
chignon	A roll of natural or artificial hair worn at back of head, 1783 onwards.
coiled	Lock of hair twisted and arranged in a circular shape.
crimping	Tight curls.
Cringle	Short hair set in upward sweeping waves, 1930s.
curl	Strands of hair twisted in a circular fashion.
Eton crop	Hair cut above ears and very short at back, 1920s and 30s.
false curls	Separate curls, pinned on owner's hair.
fillet	Band of linen or silk worn around crown of head and over forehead, fourteenth and fifteenth centuries.
fontange	Named after Mlle de Fontanges, consisting of a bow tied at top of head, above which fantastic and elaborate hair-styles were worn, 1680s.

French hood	Smooth-fitting cap from which hung a hood. The front of the cap was raised and stiffened, sixteenth century.
fringe	Hair cut and worn across the forehead.
frizz	Tightly curled hair.
full-bottomed wig	Long thick wig worn by men, eighteenth century.
gable	Tudor head-dress. A hood stiffened on the crown with a pointed arch in front, rising above the forehead.
German roll	Male hair-style, cut to 15-18 cm and turned under at ends, Victorian.
hair harvest	Hair bought from country girls and peasants during spring and summer for wig-making, nineteenth century.
heart-breaker	False curl worn by women during reign of Charles II, reaching to neck.
heart-shaped head-dress	A development from the horned head-dress, fifteenth century. The two horns protruded on either side of the head, with veils attached.
hedgehog	Hair frizzed in many tight short curls and scraped back in a ball, eighteenth century.
hennin	Tall cone-shaped head-dress, fifteenth century.
hood	Soft head-covering falling around neck and shoulders.
horned head-dress	Mediaeval head-dress. Padded horns with wires carrying a veil.
Incroyable	A dandy at the time of the French Revolution who wore long untidy hair, looking completely dishevelled.
lock	Strand of fairly long hair that hangs together; a tress.
love-lock	A long curl on the left side of the face, usually of false hair. Introduced during reign of James I.
Madonna	Short hair parted in centre with two rolls of curls, 1930s.
Marcel wave	First example of hair waved and not frizzed, nineteenth century.
Merveilleuse	Female counterpart of the Incroyable.
mingle	Short hair-style but long enough to wave and set, 1930s.
page boy	Long straight hair, turned under at ends, 1940s.
periwig	Wig of human or horse hair, thick and curled. The head was usually shaved. Male, eighteenth century.
plait	Hair divided into three and woven under and over.
Pompadour	Hair-style named after Mme de Pompadour, eighteenth century. Front hair padded, initially with wool, to raise it high above the forehead.
pony tail	Hair, usually long, tied at centre back of head and hanging down straight.
poodle	Another name for the hedgehog, eighteenth century.
poodle cut	*See* urchin cut.
razor cut	*See* urchin cut.
ringlet	A long curl, hanging vertically on the head.
roll	Hair turned up over forehead, or an artificial pad over which to turn the hair.
ruff	Circular pleated collar, sixteenth and seventeenth centuries.
scatterbrain	Mass of curls, dressed to look informal, eighteenth century.

shingle	Short straight hair, cut shorter at back, 1920s and 30s.
sugar loaf	Development of heart-shaped head-dress. Gradually turned into heart-shaped rolls, fifteenth century.
tonsure	Wig made to cover only bald parts of the head.
top knot	Hair taken to top of head and tied in a knot.
toupee	A half wig which covers the top of the head. At one time it meant the front part of a man's hair-style, often of false hair.
tower	Half wig for partly bald men, eighteenth century.
transformation	A pad of hair put under real hair to raise it, twentieth century. Or a small wig or switch of false hair, Victorian.
transplant	Method of putting new hair into scalp to cure baldness, twentieth century.
urchin cut	Hair cut short in varying lengths and brushed forward from crown, 1950s.
veil	Net or lace worn to cover face or hair.
water-waving	Hair pinched into shape when wet and set for drying, 1920s.
wave	Hair curving up and down across the head, like the sea.
wig	False hair, either human or animal, which conceals owner's hair beneath.
wimple	Piece of linen or silk wound under chin and around neck and attached to hair on top of head, fourteenth and fifteenth centuries.
Windblown	Hair dressed and set to look windswept, 1930s.

Guide to Further
Reading

Francois Boucher,
A History of Costume in the West,
Thames & Hudson, 1967

Richard Corson,
Fashions in Hair,
Peter Owen, 1965

J. S. Cox (Ed),
Hair and Beauty Secrets of Queen Victoria's Reign,
Toucan Press, 1977

Elizabeth Ewing,
History of Twentieth Century Fashion,
Batsford, 1974

G. A. Foan,
The Art and Craft of Hairdressing,
New Era, 1936

Margot Lister,
Costume,
Herbert Jenkins, 1967

Alan Mansfield and Phillis Cunningham,
Handbook of English Costume in the Twentieth Century,
Faber, 1973

Q. M. Sutton,
Headdresses of the Victorian Era,
1897

Marina Thaine and Robert Griffin,
Working in Hairdressing,
Batsford, 1980

Index

The numbers in **bold type** refer to the figure numbers of the illustrations